Praise for *Exquisite by September*

Family, food, art, activism: There's an exotic sensualness threading the poems in Hawkins' outstanding collection. Hawkins skillfully balances moments of deep pleasure, love, and beauty with harsh societal realities in a truly exquisite collection you will not want to miss.

— DIANE DECILLIS, author of *Strings Attached*
and *When the Heart Needs a Stunt Double*

Shayla Hawkins offers us many reasons to fall in love with poetry again: her lyrics are spare, unaffected and deeply felt. They know how to sing to us, how to awaken the poetry in each of us. *Exquisite by September* is exquisite every day, connecting readers to language and to one another with precise, surprising and powerful lines.

— MARILYN KALLET, author of *Even When We Sleep*
and *How Our Bodies Learned*

Exquisite by September takes us to real and imagined places where all our senses are aroused and ordinary experiences are bathed in the lush light of imagery and metaphor. We're invited to feel more deeply a first kiss, the resonance of words, the presence of a ghost; to hear the sounds beneath a song, to draw new meanings from a painting and find new ways to savour "the rip tide and rapture of [our] flesh."

— TANYA SHIRLEY, author of *She Who Sleeps with Bones*
and *The Merchant of Feathers*

Raised in Motown, molded by the music of its Electrifying Mojo, Hawkins unapologetically revels in what is elicited in so many of us by the shadows cast by parabola and curve—she extends to us, at the very least, a merciful sympathy for how it moves us to song. This collection reflects on how the softness of a grandmother is as much a story of her breasts as her kiss; reminds us that Jesse Johnson was worthy of peerage, if not a prince; recalls the tectonics of tongues "licked like a needle on a record." Her candor is a declaration that she is privy to the "pretenses of our decorum." Paddle "the shallow waters of respectability" if you want to, but Shayla Hawkins ain't the one.

— CEDRIC TILLMAN, author of *Lilies in the Valley*
and *In My Feelins*

Exquisite by September

poems

Shayla Hawkins

EASTOVER
— PRESS —
ROCHESTER, MASSACHUSETTS
www.EastOverPress.com

EXQUISITE BY SEPTEMBER

Shayla Hawkins

POETRY

© 2022

ISBN 978-1-958094-06-8

~

BOOK & COVER DESIGN: EK Larken
FRONT COVER IMAGE: Rao Bravo
AUTHOR PHOTO: Samuel L. Johnson

~

~

EastOver Press encourages the use of our publications
in educational settings. For questions about educational discounts,
contact us online: www.EastOverPress.com or info@EastOverPress.com.

PUBLISHED IN THE UNITED STATES OF AMERICA BY

Rochester, Massachusetts
www.EastOverPress.com

For Delphine Hurst Hawkins,
my beloved grandmother,
and Tressie Iola Colston,
my stylish auntie extraordinaire,
who, though they have departed this Earth,
still guide and watch over me
like the immortal exquisites they are.

CONTENTS

~Part I~

~Part II~

~Part III~

~

~

Part I

~

Bosoms

Wherever her spirit now dwells
may my grandmother laugh and be blessed
for teaching me
one childhood summer day
a lesson neither she knew
she was instructing
nor I knew
I was learning

When, between "The Price is Right"
and her religiously watched soap operas,
we sat to lunch in her dining room
and my grandmother,
with no more thought
than if she had pushed down
two flour sacks,
grabbed her colossal breasts
and tucked them neatly
under the table
so she could reach her plate

My grandmother,
whose bosom had suckled and comforted
five children plus a husband
and looked like two watermelons on steroids,
showed me in that one swift move
that breasts are not to be envied,
worshipped or feared,
that for all their cultural succulence
and mammary goodness,
sometimes a woman's bosom
is nothing less or more

than a fleshy nuisance
to be pushed into the shadows
so she can sip her sweet tea in peace
and savor her chicken soup with rice

A Beckoning

My and my grandmother's dreams
meet in time's continuum

Rescinded from death,
pulled back in age
to the Ontario home of her birth,
she reclines one August afternoon
on her bed and stares out her window

A southern wind
rolls over the Detroit River
and sighs through her linen curtains

She sighs also,
and breathes me, not yet born,
into her body,
my demons and wishes
writhing in her chest,

my restless spirit
mingled with her own,
my formless self
looking through her eyes
past Amherstburg's main road
to the edge of town
with its lush farming fields
and farther north to Michigan,

bewitched like her
by the waving columns of wheat
that sway and curl
like a siren's fingers,
a beckoning

to dance and drink in the sun's
heady gold light
with no mention of its waning
or the soon-coming night

Roses

after Lawrence Alma-Tadema's The Roses of Heliogabalus

As clever as she was in life
so she remained after death,
my grandmother,
whose ghost one day
for no apparent reason
visited—no, washed over—me
in the checkout line
at Kroger

Her spirit smelling
like every rose
of Eden,
Xanadu,
and Shangri-La,
so overflowing
with her favorite scent
that it cascaded onto me
as I stood unsuspecting
among racks of tabloids,
bubble gum, and beef jerky

A floral perfume
flooding my nostrils,
streaming like ribbons
from my fingertips until I felt
as if I had been dipped
and rolled and smothered
in roses

Almost like the victims
of Heliogabalus,
crazed Roman emperor

with death's gallows written
into his very name,
fabled to have suffocated
his banquet guests beneath
a cataclysm of falling roses
for no reason other than
because he could

But where he
used roses as a weapon,
my grandmother
used them for wisdom,
to show me that,
alive or dead,
there is no time or place,
not even a Tuesday afternoon
at a supermarket,
where she
cannot reach me,
where she cannot wrap
me in love as fragrant and soft
as a rose-scented blanket
for no reason other than
because she can

Orchids in Cienfuegos

slim, green-stemmed
muchachos and mamacitas
capped in fragrant yellow fedoras
and white petal mantillas

tropical columnata
dancing the Conga
while the wind
plays invisible timbales

sinuous orchids
rooted in rhythm
sweat their sweet vanilla musk
and sway and bob their bright heads
as if to say
yes to the sun and sea
yes to the riot of beauty
and revolution birthed
from the same suelo santo
this wild
this holy
Cuba earth

Scent of Eden

Humid April nights
smell like a just-showered man:
citrus, hint of musk,
sweet melon fresh from the vine,
scent of Earth, scent of Eden

Eating Paradise

*"Guayaba is pronounced guava in English. As the story goes,
perfection and heaven made love and conceived the first guayaba."*
~ *Francisco Pino*

Saturday breakfast
and we eat paradise
disguised as guayaba

Its tropic flavor
sweet, congealed
Its smooth, contained coolness
this morning's
edible opposite
of last night's slippery
heat and love

Lush, fruit-laden symbol of flesh
and our rest afterwards
when my body
still warm and sparkling
with your sweat
slumbered atop
the cotton sheets
like sliced guava
laid on Spanish bread
and you leaned into the dark
to kiss my neck

Like a wasp
that temporarily relinquishes
its sting
to descend and drink
nectar from an orchid
wrapped in rain
and the night's
long ebony shadows

Vanilla

The word "vanilla" comes from the Spanish word "vainilla"
(meaning "little pod") which itself is descended from the
Latin word for "sheath": "vagina."

a silver teaspoon
of Pure Bourbon Madagascar Vanilla

not a lot
but enough
to lift my mind
from my American kitchen
and wrap my senses
in its African island sweetness

enough for its heady orchid fragrance
to cling to that spoon
hours later
and carry me back
to the memory of you
and your body
spooned with my body

the frames of our flesh
bending and fitting themselves
to fill and fulfill
each other's need

you me us
two seeds of vanilla
in our own little pod
pressed together
until we yield and spill
our own hypnotic pleasures
too sweet
for our bodies
to contain

Butter Pecan

smooth confluence
of sugar butter
nuts cream
this delectable dream
churned into real-life lusciousness

salty sweet delicious
chunky pecan crunch
milky mound that enters frozen
into my mouth
then melts in a pool
of liquid pleasure

ambrosial marriage of flavors
tangy sweetness so exquisite
that with each taste
all my body rejoices
even my tongue
speaks in tongues

Pot Au Chocolat

"Chocolate pots are distinguished by a hole in the lid where a stirring rod could be inserted."
    ~ *Taylor Newby, Metropolitan Museum of Art*

Some nights
like this night

an invisible flint
sparks a kindling
between us
that sends our bodies
beyond words
shapes them
into symbols
and poetry itself

My hips
my behind
my belly and thighs
paired with the exquisite
almost unbearable
nearness of you
become a feminine
French metaphor
replicating the curves
and silver sheen
of a chocolate pot
whose hidden sweetness
melts at your touch
and the lush
lean length
of your phallus
and your physique
become my stirring rod

most welcome agitator
rising, gravity-defying
flesh stick
aimed and sliding
into me

pulsing churning spinning
a delicious liquefaction
of pleasure
greater than even the sum
of our poetic selves
can express

Mocha Brown

for Sam

He called
the color of my voice
mocha brown

Deeper than caramel,
he said,
but richer and sweeter
than coffee

A voice
whose liquid-like earthiness
can be imbibed
and savored
and linger
in a listener's mind
long after its sound
has left his ear

How then could I not delight
in such a description
from such a man
who used his own voice,
the soft silvery dark
of dew on a morning glory,
to call forth magic and light
from something of mine
so familiar
that, until him,
I dismissed it
as ordinary

Aling

aling [Hindi], noun: embrace

Our embrace has become its own wheel and world,
A two-bodied braid of bone and fire.
At your touch the scroll of passion unfurls.
Our embrace has become its own wheel and world.

Chakra and flesh into a chasm hurled
Of love and excruciating desire.
Our embrace has become its own wheel and world,
A two-bodied braid of bone and fire.

Haunt

Handsome, irresistible
unholy ghost
far from me as eternity
yet like eternity so close

Undressing me in my dreams
with your supernatural gaze
then dissolving into stardust
with a shadowy haze

Warrior ghost mighty enough
to invade my heart and head,
be man enough to materialize
and lay yourself in my bed

Quiet Kinks

"Why are the quiet ones always the kinkiest?" ~ *Mitchell Royel*

I can't speak
for the multitude
of my quiet kindred
but I can tell you this:

Why waste my breath talking
when there are so many more
pleasant things to blow
than hot air?

Why litter the air
with the clutter of chatter
when I speak
the erotic unspeakable
more eloquently
with my eyes
tongue, teeth and, yes,
even my toes?

My silent sisters can confirm:
language is good
but gets you only so far
and what words
can describe that feeling
when a lover's breath
lands soft and exotic
as a peacock's feather
between their breasts?

My wallflower brothers
could tell you:
talk has its time and place
but words have no power
over that certain glance
from that certain someone
that gets them
long and stiff
as a stiletto

So there lies your answer

We quiet ones
have mastered the art
of "Show, Don't Tell"
and know instinctively
when to keep our mouths shut
and when
where
and for whom
to open them

The Mango Virgin

He stood on Prince George Wharf
selling mangoes.
I walked apart from the crowd,
yet he knew I was a tourist.

He pointed at me. "You," he said. "Come here."
I heard the whisper of chimes
and Bahamian sea in his voice. I obeyed.
"You never ate a mango, young mama?"
My tongue grew heavy in his presence.
I shook my head. His lips parted
to a gap-toothed smile.

"Such a shame," he laughed.
"You can do many things with a mango."
The sun threw a slanted gleam
over his salt-and-pepper beard.
He lifted a knife from his cart
then joined the blade to a mango.
Its flesh hissed as it shaped itself
to the knife's rhythm, its juices snaking
down the man's arm.

When he finished, the mango slice lay
atop the knife, both bodies
glistening. He lifted the fruit
with his dark brown fingers to my mouth.
"Eat," he coaxed.
"You be a mango virgin no more."

The fruit slipped over my lips. I swallowed,
sweetness bathing my tongue and teeth.
I reached into my purse to pay.

"No charge, m'lady. When you learn the mango's secrets,
you come back to see me." He winked.

I walked away.
The sidewalks changed to clouds,
the human throngs to forests.
I brought the mango to my mouth
and sucked it softly.
I felt like the first woman
tasting God's tongue.

Drink

after Jan Vermeer's The Glass of Wine

Notice the clever way
the woman's cap
conceals her face
at the same time
her wine glass reveals it

Now look at the man
looking at her
drinking in her features
as if her eyes, her cheeks,
her lips themselves
were a full-bodied Chablis
and his cloaked body
the cask and bottle designed
to cradle and pour out
every drop
of her sweetness

Swallow

after Jan Vermeer's The Procuress

The root meaning of her title—
"to care for"—
and what she actually does
are so opposite
that you might laugh

But your laughter
might die in your throat
when you really see
the money-mangled gleam
in her aged eyes,
the lecherous slink
of the one man's smile,
and the massive, bear-like hand of the john
already clawing the brightly clad
hooker's breast

Then there's the hooker herself,
her young hand unfurling like a flower,
taking the gold shimmer
of the john's coin
as easily as she will soon swallow
her glass of liquor, her pride,
and other dangerous things

~
Part II
~

Cage

after Jean-Léon Gérôme's Pool in a Harem

Look how she bends
to speak
and they lean in
to listen

Their stark differences—
her creased ebony face,
hoop earring half hidden
in the shadows between
her neck and dark blue burqa
mere inches from their
creamy alabaster skin
and pink-tipped breasts—
somehow balanced
and brought into focus
in the harem's humid mist

The red-haired courtesan
perched on a satin pillow,
fingering the lapis beads
of a necklace,
her bare behind
like a moon gleaming
against blue marble tile

The brunette, sitting upright
on a Turkish rug,
her legs and lower chest wrapped
in a bath sheet,
small flower bright
as a blood drop
pinned in her hair

Both of them
looking at this servant,
attentive to her words
and not the hookahs she holds
in her dark calloused hands

If they are not friends,
they certainly are companions
in each other's fates,
sharers of news that illumines
their knowledge of the outside world
like the ceiling skylights
piercing the harem's wet heat
with feathery glints of sun

The black slave
the two concubines
the ghostlike odalisques
in the background haze,
all linked as women
whose lives are not their own,
like a raven and a flock of doves
tethered to the same
gilded cage

Glittering Whip

for Mia, the Egyptian cobra that escaped her enclosure at the Bronx Zoo
and was found six days later resting in a dark corner

glittering whip
curled in darkness

ophidian twist
of muscle
and patterned skin
curving
around walls
like a cocktail dress
sliding down
a woman's body

sexy
lethal as sin
oh reptilian professor
the classes you could teach
on power
and seduction

the stories
your forked tongue
could tell

how with equal ease
your quiet venom
can puncture
Cleopatra's breast
and make
a concrete American jungle
tremble
in its skyscraper armor
at the mere mention
of your name

Medusa Instructs the New Cosmetologist

My hair be a snake bush
a hydra-headed hurricane
whirling
writhing
in its raw power

Hear that hiss?
That's not an apology
or a plea for you to accept
and understand me

Those be the serpent sisters
on my scalp
dishing you fair warning
that if you play the fool with me
it will be at your peril
and telling you too
that my tresses
are to be trimmed
not tamed
styled
not stifled

But don't be scared
They won't bite
unless they have to
and their venom stings
but almost never kills

So just breathe
Relax
Take your time
Work your magic

Sugar Fire

*"Etta could sing the Sears catalog and make you want to
buy every item."* ~ *Marvin Gaye on Etta James*

Had she taken a shine to it,
no doubt she could have sung
the praises and practical benefits
of screwdrivers, table napkins,
pantyhose

But Etta's business
was the heart
with all its magic and mess,
her mission like love itself:
impossible, immaculate

Yet somehow
with her jazzy honky-tonk
and bluesy gutbucket growl
Etta accomplished the task,
singing her soul
until the sound
poured like sugar and fire
from her blonde bouffant head,
her music a sweet, hot cleansing
that made equals of all lovers:
the jilted, the wishful,
the blessed and the badass

Etta's grooves and ballads
a melodic mirror
where if only for a spell
folks could find
reflection and rest
before tumbling headlong again
into love's brutal,
luscious thunder

Mojo Working

Detroit, Michigan, circa 1980

Rhythm pulling me
like a magnet to the door
outside my father's den
and The Electrifying Mojo,
deejay of deejays,
talking smooth
and deep as thunder,
comes through the radio
and music
rides the lush carpet
of his voice
straight into my heart

Soul, techno, rock, R&B
Mojo doesn't care:
If it's good, he spins it
and tonight he's spinning
"I Wanna Be Your Lover"
by some new cat
from Minnesota called Prince

This guy I think
must be nuts,
putting all his business
out in the street, singing sexy
over keyboards, bass, and guitar
to a woman about things
my crayon-wielding Kindergarten self
isn't supposed to know,
yet somehow I do

And I get so caught up
in the lovecrazy magic
of this song that I think for a moment
it's possible to crawl through
my daddy's stereo

to WGPR on East Jefferson
where Mojo's in his studio
working the records
that drip a honey-sweet funk
into my ears
and thank him
for planting a wish
in my little girl heart
to be a woman
and have a man
singing to her
with all the passion
of that looney dude
from Minneapolis

Say Yes

for Jesse Johnson

After he sings, the handsome
funk-rock guitarist sits
for an interview on "The Scene,"
the Detroit TV dance show
that my six-year-old self
watches from home
as he reclines in front of the set's
silver spangled backdrop,
a bevy of beautiful black women
fawning over him, the show's emcee asking him
standard questions
about his group's newest album,
their next tour,
how he's handling his success

But then the emcee hands the mic
to one of the fawning women
whose question is anything but typical:
"Can I kiss you?"
She asks, giggling, as the other women
laugh and clap and scream,
wishing they had her nerve

And Jesse Johnson,
with his soft, deep voice;
his immaculate jheri curl
that amazingly drips no activator
on his custom-made suit;
and his bright brown eyes
twinkling like two of the 11,000 lakes
in his adopted home state of Minnesota,
agrees and, like it's just another day

at the office, leans in and gives this bold
and most blessed among women
not a peck on her cheek,
but a full-bodied lip-lock

so lush and magnetic

it almost sucks me through the TV,
leaving me breathless and blinking
in a jaw-dropping daze
that my elementary school mind
doesn't have the language to describe

Yet, still, instinctively I know
this will shape me, this moment
when I see something impossible come to life
because of a woman confident enough
to ask for what she wants
and a man generous enough
to say yes

Record

Ten years later, I can laugh
at how I started out dreading
the night I got my first French kiss,
laugh, too, at how nervous I was with my date, with myself,
how I didn't trust the chemistry
that crackled and burned between us like a lava flow,
how, when he smiled at me in the restaurant,
I had to stop my head from swiveling
to make sure there wasn't a better, prettier woman behind me

But then, when I remember him driving me home,
I stop laughing and my body gets quiet and warm,
just like it did in his car after I made some corny joke
about love at first sight and he pulled into the driveway and said,
"It wasn't love at first sight, but I love you now."

And I remember his glance hot and soft
as a September sun on my face
and how I knew he was telling the truth,
our attraction so palpable not even my favorite
Mariah Carey remix playing on his car stereo
could distract me from it, and how my breath
seemed to get tangled in my lungs
but it didn't matter because suddenly his mouth
was on my mouth, my soul pulled into the pink suction
of his lips, my nose filled with the musk
and sandalwood scent of his cologne,
my awkwardness slipping away from me
like lingerie liberated in his hands
as he guided my hands to the muscles
beneath his respectable khaki shirt,
his tongue touching my tongue,
licking like a needle on a record,

patiently probing and circling as I licked him back,
my rigid black curves spinning and flaring
into a love song as primal and erotic
as the pulsing between my thighs

Treasure

after Vievee Francis's Epicurean

A broad chest, a barrel chest, chest that Atlas
wished to have before he hefted the world's weight
onto his shoulders. A chest that I would fill
with the pearls and gold doubloons of my love,
that I would fight Ali Baba and the 40 thieves
to take as my own. A chest whose sublime musculature
Michelangelo, even with the finest Carrara marble,
would be hard-pressed to chisel and replicate

Not the mothball-laden metal chest of my childhood
where wool blankets and winter socks were kept,
but a chest of blood and bone and flesh
that, from neck to navel, my lips would kiss clean each night.
In my adoration, I would have this chest, enter with reverence
its cave of wonders, both losing and finding myself
there in the riches of my beloved's secrets, the breath of his life,
and, the greatest treasure, his heart.

Mademoiselle Blue

after Henri Matisse's Blue Nude III

I.
sinuous blue curves
fluid motion in stillness
voluptuous grace

II.
a mark of genius:
to cut blue paper until
a woman bursts forth

III.
three blue mysteries:
the ocean, the endless sky,
this serene woman

IV.
shapely blue music
this curious cut-out both
plain and exotic

V.
Oh, Mademoiselle Blue,
what dreams, riddles, and longings
lurk beneath your skin

Butler's Magic

after Joseph DeCamp's The Steward (El Mayordomo)

In this job
appearance
is everything

Decorum and neatness
are next to God

So I have learned
to conceal
my real self

as easily as I bind
my bowtie
to my neck

as smoothly
as I polish silver
until it shines like blood
in the sunlight

Yes
this job
is a great teacher
and I am a diligent student

I have learned
that you
can get away
with almost anything
if you dress it up
pretty enough

Take the pig
on this platter
for instance

Golden
roasted to perfection

so succulent and crisp
you can almost
taste it
devour it

and not once think
of its slaughter

That's the magic
of my work

to play sleight-of-hand
with light and dark
perception and reality

to serve a slashed creature
so skillfully
that it looks delicious
and your curiosity
concerning its scars
disappears

The Devil's Work

Bicycles
hula hoops
jigsaw puzzles
plush bears
the unconquerable
fuchsia-boxed queendom
of Barbie dolls

That trip
to the toy store
that day
the same as any other

Until I drifted away
from my mother
to the game row
and my fingers found a Ouija board

Its heft and cryptic calligraphy
calling me
its slickly packaged promise
to make me
a telepathic transcriber
a sort-of secretary to the dead
singing to me
sweet and seductive
as the serpent and fruit
that bewitched Eve
naked and foolish to her doom

But for the child I was that day
a curiosity forever unfulfilled
because of a mother

who walked up to me cool and quiet
as graveyard fog
snatched the game
from my hands
and warned me never
to touch it again

Don't play
with the devil's work
she said and steered me
to the exit doors
away from the moment
where I wondered if I
like the board I had just held
possessed untapped
powers forbidden
or if the stirrings of my heart
were little more
than a parlor trick
sheathed in sepia skin
and shadows

Mama Leviathan

North Coast, Tortola, British Virgin Islands

Her presence
starts a prickle in my neck
electric spine-tingling telling me
something in the Carib fathoms
is watching me

And just beneath the boat
there she is
a humpback whale
slow torpedo in the silver azure sea
the gaze of her gray eye
smooth as glass
bold as her barnacles are bumpy

Calf on her back
she breaks the surface
mama leviathan and child
breathe with a rumbling hiss
that shoots rainbow sprays
from their spouts

Twice more
then she slips with her baby
back below the waters
leaving me in her wake
grateful that she spared
the full brunt of power
that would surely have killed me
and chose instead
to greet me and depart
with the same serene grace

that sounds even now in my blood
the way her songs echo
through the blue
and billowing deep

In Brussels

The tour maps and brochures make no mention
of all the black people in Belgium,
the immigrants and their descendants
from Rwanda, Burundi, the Congo,
who came here after fleeing
wars, massacres and famines,
after King Leopold II
stripped their lands of diamonds
just as fast as he could steal them.

Nobody tells me that the first person
I'll see in Brussels
will be a black man standing at a bus stop,
or that the concierge and half the restaurant staff
at my hotel was born in Kinshasa.

My travel book does not inform me
that later, on a night tour of the city,
with the lilt of French and Flemish words
and the fragrance of chocolate
and sugar-scented waffles floating on the air,
I'll be in the cobblestone square
of the Grand-Place and see a black woman
with skin the color of clover honey
and an afro of strawberry blonde corkscrew curls.

No one tells me that when she sees me looking at her,
she'll smile and say, "Ça va, ma sœur,"
("What's up, my sister") then walk on,
her suede leather coat and flame-red hair
sailing past me and my preconceived notions
like a comet blazing through the starlit, indigo night.

Show Up

how do i still see so clearly 30 years later
how he slid from behind the dumpster
that night at the gas station on eight mile

creepy quiet trouble man
bad vibe blaring from him
like times square neon

my godmother at the gas pump
filling her tank
after the friday night revival
at our church that went on so long
it put her two sons to sleep
who were still slumbering
mouths open softly snoring
next to me in the back seat of her car

but i was wide awake watching
the shadow come out
shapeshift in the dark
cloak himself in a man's skin
baggy jeans jacket gym shoes

growing taller bolder
more solid and ruthless
with each step he takes towards us

his eyes a laser on my godmother
his footsteps finally close enough
for her to turn and see him

in these last seconds
before he pulls and aims
the loaded weight in his jacket
before my godmother can scream
before everything
changes and shatters

another car pulls into the station
another man three times the menace's size
hops out and with a fearlessness
known only to muscle-strapped dudes
starts filling his tank at the pump
next to us

and just that fast the shadow steps back
runs towards eight mile
melts into the night

all i can do is stare astonished
at the big bowlegged angel
for stopping the gun i never saw
the shots i never heard
the blood that was not shed
all because he picked this moment
to show up

Voyeur

after Edgar Degas's The Tub

Here is where a woman's bathing
becomes a force
primal, scorching as fire
that turns a painter
on the verge of blindness and death
into a voyeur
and makes
a younger man's passion
surge like a maple's sap
in his withered bones

Here is that old man's
ribald understanding
that if he cannot physically
caress that bathing woman,
he still can paint his yearning
so palpable that it pulses
on the canvas
and becomes a lurking
that illumines
and washes her body,
closer even
than the water and light
on her skin

Lettuce

From her nervous chirp
of laughter
to the skin and bone fingers
that lift like an egret's wing
and push into her mouth
one piece of lettuce
watery and frail
as her smile,
she almost could be a bird

And by the cautious way
she nibbles the wilted leaf,
eyes darting and alert
as she sits opposite
two muscle-strapped
teenage boys
who tear like wolves
into their meat sandwiches,
she almost could be a rabbit

But instead she is
heartbreakingly human,
her young face
creased already
with self-doubt
and the caustic knowledge
of America's impossible
synthetic standards
of female beauty,
feeding only her hunger
with each soft bite
of salad she takes,
this teenage girl,
who almost could be a woman

By the Skin of Her Teeth

after Edgar Degas's Miss La La at the Cirque Fernando

Who knows where
along America's eastern shore
she departed

Perhaps Savannah
with its King Cotton warehouses
and cobblestone pier

Maybe she slipped
through Baltimore's
fried clam and crab cake air

Who's to say she didn't embark
from New York City's
teeming human tide

But wherever she left
there's no doubt where she arrived

For by the time Degas sees her,
she is Miss La La,
acrobatic Parisian wonder

Her black American
name and existence scratched off
like a bothersome scab

And in their place
a luminous brown woman
spinning like a spangled star
high in the rafters
of the most famous circus in Paris

By the time Degas
immortalizes Miss La La with his paint

she has perfected
her own art
of perilous brilliance

her circus act distilling the dangers
of a 19th century
black woman's life

the tightly clenched rope
in Miss La La's mouth
symbol and testimony

of her ability
to survive
by the skin of her teeth

to seize
the death-defying beauty
of dangling from a big-top ceiling

and turn it into
a twirling dizzying shimmer
of hypnotic grace

~
Part III
~

Daughter, Deliverer

*During one of her last trips on the Underground Railroad,
Harriet Tubman returned to her native Maryland and rescued
her own parents from slavery.*

As you once birthed me from blood into light,
tonight I return the favor.
You delivered me from darkness to life.
Only you can call me daughter.

Tonight I return your favor.
Some call me Moses, Redeemer, North Star.
But only you can call me daughter.
So I pay you back with freedom.

Others call me Moses, Redeemer, North Star.
Tomorrow let Massa wake to find you gone
and see that I've paid you back with freedom.
But tonight, let us run while he dreams.

Tomorrow, Massa will wake and find you gone.
You delivered me. From darkness to life,
tonight we will run while he dreams,
as you once birthed me from blood into light.

The Circle

"Will the circle be unbroken, by and by, Lord, by and by?"
~ traditional gospel hymn

An unbroken circle
of black bodies broken
in American streets
turned to winding sheets

Michael Brown
the circle's latest member
a black kid vibrant
with teenage bravado
until he met a cop's ammunition

Each bullet
a horizontal neutron bomb
bursting his organs
blasting apart his bones

until his ruined body
like that officer's bullets
became just another shell
that fell to the street

his soul slipping out of his flesh
like his blood
looking down
at his own mangled corpse
left to lie for four hours
in Missouri's August heat

wondering how he
so recently filled with life
and flaws and a future
so suddenly became
a ghost at the end
of a white man's gun

but no one
can hear his questions
and no one
answers them

So Michael Brown
has no choice
but to take his place
in the deadly ring
of murdered
and unavenged black lives
where he sees

Trayvon Martin
and Eric Garner

Emmett Till
and Oscar Grant

Sean Bell

Amadou Diallo

and they swap stories
and wait in dread
for the circle's next member

whose face
whose life
whose death
whose killer

will be different
and yet
so much
like their own

Witness

for Darnella Frazier

she does not yet know
that this street outside this store
will become a black man's middle passage
from life to brutal death
his crucible and Via Dolorosa

his journey
on his people's ancient path of sorrows
ending here on the concrete
under the merciless 8 minutes and 46 seconds
of a white cop's knee on his neck
as three more cops do nothing
but watch him die

she does not yet know as she records
the scene with her cell phone
that she is cementing her place
in the sacred, horrific royal lineage
of black girls and women bearing witness
to the murder of brothers husbands
sons complete strangers

or that by the time she is finished
and the black man facedown on the ground
has cried out for his mother
and the last of his oxygen
has left his crushed lifeless body
they will no longer be strangers

but she his sister
he her brother
giving her his stolen breath
her taking it to show the last testament of his life
the casual savagery of his killing

and ignite a revolution
throughout this plague-ravaged planet
for justice and reparation
for him and all
their brothers and sisters

R.I.P. George Floyd, October 14, 1973 – May 25, 2020

Spirit Mother

after Paul Gauguin's The Ancestors of Tehamana

Tehamana, Gauguin's kept and colonized Tahitian woman,
stares from his painting in constricting European clothes
as if she knows that her fate will be like the flowers in her hair:
a fading, slow wilting into oblivion,
and that her dreams, like the mangoes at her side, are destined
to grow no sweeter or go any further than the confines of his canvas

But one of her spirit mothers, Hina, goddess of the moon,
stands bare-breasted in the background, prepared to fight all of this,
her face painted red, her arms raised and ready for war,
her legs splayed like she's about to leap into the future,
snatch the fan from her spirit daughter's hand,
and whip her complacency into a raging flame

Beautiful Botany

Early May
and the neighbor's magnolia tree
just beyond the bathroom window
has started to unfold
its fragrant pink-white petals
while just inside
of that bathroom window
my prepubescent self
gazes in a mirror
at her body's changing topography
takes inventory
of her bony, rock-like knees
the valley of her pubis,
the straight lines of her hips
just starting to bend
into their curves

But mostly she squints
with her near-sighted eyes
at the two little peaks
that seem to have sprung up overnight
on her chest,
scrutinizing them and their glass reflection,
wondering when they will transform
from small buds into feminine
magnificent milk-filled breasts

And I look through the decades
back at her
back at me
and want to laugh
and tell this child

to take her eagerness down a notch,
to trust the strange, beautiful botany

of her body
and know that
in their own perfect time
her breasts will ripen
and flower like the roses
and tulips and magnolias
just beyond
the bathroom window

Drift

Like a parachute
that almost
but not quite opens

Or a paste-on smile
that almost
but not quite reaches my eyes

So is my sympathy
for those poor intimidated souls
who call themselves
enlightened
until innocently confronted
by the natural largesse
of my chest

And then
despite themselves
cannot stop the downward drift
of their eyes
to my décolletage

Until like skin divers
their gaze plummets
into the fully clothed
curves and crests of my cleavage

Until I can almost
hear them drowning
in my full-breasted bounty
flowing with then fighting
their peaks and swells

Until at last delivered
by some remembered pretense
of decorum
they stop their naked staring

and are pulled
from the rip tide and rapture
of my flesh
and paddle the shallow waters
of respectability
back to safety

Tressie Iola

One May Saturday you told Tressie Iola,
your mother's most beautiful sister
with the country bumpkin name but
the glamorous cinnamon beige skin
and hazel eyes, how you couldn't wait
to grow up and get married and have kids

And that same Tressie Iola, who told
your nine-year-old self how to blot
lipstick with tissue to make it last longer
even though you weren't allowed to wear it
for the next seven years and described her most favorite,
effervescent New Year's Eve champagne
even though your parents didn't drink

Looked at you with those flashing copper green eyes
over her frothy cup of some multisyllabic Italian coffee
and told you with the hard-earned wisdom of a woman
who turned down a modeling career that would have
taken her to New York City and Milan
to be a wife and mother in Detroit,
"Girl, one thing there will always be plenty of is sperm.
Put that stuff on the back burner and go live your life."
And every spring after that,
when the dandelion blooms danced

and white petal arabesques of apple blossoms
and green maple tree seedlings
filled and fell from the sky
like a botanical version of Magritte's
bowler-hatted raining men,
you delighted in their flight but waved them on
and wished them and all the plentiful sperm of the world

happy travels
because you were not waiting for them
to fill you with magic
because you were living your life and learning
that you are your own magic

Exquisite by September

Belle Isle, Detroit, Michigan, Summer 1976

my mother turns her face
from the camera
aimed at her pregnant profile
stares into the sunlit distance
at something only she can see

her gaze dreamy and calm
her maternity blouse
billowing from her belly
as if the wind itself has stolen
a glimpse inside her mind
and sighs with pleasure at her thoughts

whoever holds the camera
takes my mother's picture anyway
immortalizing her rare serenity
at the same moment it is invaded
capturing her contemplation
there at the water's edge
and the waxing crescent moon of her stomach

my mother
a human tree
radiant in the peach August light
and I the fleshy fruit
nestled inside of her
stretching, growing
biding my time
like a harvest apple
to drop into the world
birthed into the fullness of myself
ruddy and sweet
and exquisite by September

ABOUT THE POET

SHAYLA HAWKINS is a Detroit native, poet, and writer whose works have been in *Calabash, Crab Orchard Review, tongues of the ocean, The Taj Mahal Review,* and *Poets & Writers,* among other publications. She is a Cave Canem founding fellow and has been a featured reader at the Geraldine R. Dodge Poetry Festival and the Library of Congress. She also is a past winner of The Caribbean Writer's Canute A. Brodhurst Prize in Short Fiction and an Archie D. & Bertha H. Walker Scholarship to the Fine Arts Work Center in Provincetown, Massachusetts.

Her first book, *Carambola*, was published in 2012 by David Robert Books. National Book Award-winning author Charles Johnson cited its poems as "deliciously sensuous, smart... vivid, and luminous with the life of the spirit...."

Hawkins has also published poems in several anthologies including *Mona Poetica*, commemorating the 500th anniversary of Leonardo DaVinci's *Mona Lisa* painting; *Chopin with Cherries*, celebrating the life and musical genius of Frederic Chopin; *Delirious: A Poetic Celebration of Prince; Joys of the Table: An Anthology of Culinary Verse; The Practicing Poet;* and *A Constellation of Kisses.*

Acknowledgements

Grateful acknowledgement is made to the editors of the following print and/or online publications in which these poems (sometimes in earlier versions) first appeared:

Blue Fifth Review and *Joys of the Table*: "Eating Paradise"

A Constellation of Kisses: "Record"

Edison Literary Review: "Glittering Whip"

Fine Arts Work Center Blog: "Bosoms"

Last Stanza Poetry Journal: "Roses"

Naugatuck River Review: "By the Skin of Her Teeth"

Saraba Magazine: "Aling"

The Caribbean Writer: "Mama Leviathan" and "Orchids in Cienfuegos"

Theodate: "Voyeur"

The Practicing Poet: "Treasure" and "Record"

The Strategic Poet: "Tressie Iola"

Tidal Basin Review: "Mojo Working" and "Daughter, Deliverer"

tongues of the ocean: "The Mango Virgin"

THANKS

Thank you to all the following who made *Exquisite by September* better than it would have been without them:

Donny, the best brother I know who inspires me every day just by being his wonderful self; Samuel L. Johnson, master poem evaluator and friend of few words who is still faithful as the sunrise and comes through for me in the clutch like Game 7 Steph Curry; Marilyn Kallet, Diane DeCillis, Cedric Tillman, and Tanya Shirley, who responded to my blurb requests with the speed of Olympic athletes. Thank you so much for believing in me and my poetry. You inspire me not just with your poems, but your great kindness as well; Rao Bravo, for gifting me with such a beautiful painting that turned out to be a perfect visual tapestry for *Exquisite by September*; Denton Loving and the entire EastOver Press staff for giving *Exquisite by September* a good home and all the work they put in to share it with the world; Jesse Johnson, for showing me that my wildest dreams can come true and that one of the world's greatest guitarists can become the inspiration for one of my most favorite poems as well as a cherished friend; my fellow introverted poets and writers, who cringe at the thought of going public with their work but know they've been called to create and bear witness through the literary arts (If my quiet self can gather enough courage and tenacity to share my poems and stories and write a book, you can, too. The world needs your words and their clarity and intensity. Get to it.); you, dear reader, for making time for *Exquisite by September*. May it inspire you to seek, find, and multiply the beauty and mystery in your own life; and, above all, to God and the Lord Jesus Christ. Thank you for the gifts of poetry, life everlasting, and your love.